GUIDED BY
GRACE

Roma MacKinnon

BALBOA.PRESS
A DIVISION OF HAY HOUSE

Balboa Press books may be ordered through booksellers or by contacting:

Balboa Press
A Division of Hay House
1663 Liberty Drive
Bloomington, IN 47403
www.balboapress.com
844-682-1282

Print information available on the last page.

ISBN: 979-8-7652-3715-1 (sc)
ISBN: 979-8-7652-3742-7 (e)

Balboa Press rev. date: 12/19/2022

CONTENTS

LIKE CRAYONS LOVE COLORING BOOKS

*T*he day is bright, the sun is awake in the sky, it's warm on my skin. I can hear the birds singing their beautiful songs, cheering each other on, backing each other up. The grass is ever so green and lush, the rain that pelts down so often helps the grass become so green. I am with my granny and my aunt Molly it's my happy place, I feel safe and loved and nurtured here.

We are going to the shops to buy a few things that we need. I'm touching the leafy bushes as we walk past them. I pick some off, swish them with my thumb and my finger and break right through them. I like how it feels. Soft and velvety, moist and dewy I'm happy. I begin to skip as I hold my granny's hand I hum a song, content in my space and place in this world.

We arrive at the shops and my granny picks out the things she needs. I'm allowed a comic a coloring book and crayons. Im in heaven. I choose what I like and we pay and walk home. It's a big walk, far for my granny and me, but we manage. I want to get back real quick. I want to do my coloring in and read my comic. But I still skip and sing and talk to my granny. She looks beautiful with her red lipstick and her hat. I love her like peanut butter loves jam, like oreas love cream, like popcorn loves butter.

When we get home I settle down with my coloring in and my granny gets busy making our tea with aunt Molly, we have our tea and relax for the night. My granny knits, I color in, aunt Molly reads the newspaper.

I'm scared to go to bed on my own, so I get to stay up. I go up to bed with aunt Molly and we get tucked in, aunt Molly hides candies under her pillow and I tell her she's going to get in trouble, we disagree, but then she offers me some, and I take them. We lie in bed talking and laughing and eating candy and I love my aunt Molly like the earth loves the rain, like a dog love a walk, like a bird loves to fly, like crayons love coloring books

I fall asleep, content, safe, peaceful, wanted, loved, safe, did I say safe. It's so safe in this house. These people love me.

THE COLD TRUTH

*I*t's a grey morning, it's autumn and I have just been dropped of at my Granny's house. The room is very still, it contains a couch and chairs, a bed in the recess, a sink, a yellow kitchen cabinet, where dishes and food are stored, a side board with a grandmother clock sitting on it. A table and chairs that gleam to a shine.

My granny lies in bed, sleeping, the fire is not lit, and I'm too young to start a fire so I sit in the chair facing the bed in the recess desperately wanting to climb in that bed with my granny. I'm freezing cold, teeth chattering. How can I find the courage to ask? She won't allow it, I won't be allowed in her bed. I've never been allowed in her bed.

I sit there in almost complete silence, listening to the grandmother clock ticking. It's the only sound in the room. I look around me at the two seater couch, but I dare not lie down there, it would be frowned upon and I would be chastised, so I continue to sit in the chair shivering, aching to be warm.

I can't speak, I'll be in big trouble if I speak, especially if I say what I want to say, which is actually a question. I feel scared, troubled, confused, sad, upset. I want to cry, but I'm not permitted to do that either, there will be trouble if I cry. So I don't I just shiver some more.

I finally find some courage, and I ask my granny "are you going to get up" she says "no" I feel panicked, terrified, what should I do now? I look at the fireplace willing it to light itself. I sit on my hands to try to warm them, I breath heavy, my anxiety is big, I'm so so scared.

It's been a long time. I know my cousin is allowed to sleep in my granny's bed, but why not me I wonder. Why does she get to climb in that bed and snuggle in and be warm and I can't. I want to ask but I can't. She'll get angry with me, she's always angry with me. So I continue to sit there on my hands as they go numb.

I'm going to cry soon I can feel it, she won't like my tears, she'll be angry at my tears so I better not cry. I bite my cheek stoping myself from wailing. I don't dare drop one tear, I have to hold my sadness, my fear, my shivering cold in. It won't go well for me if I don't.

Eventually I cannot stand the damp cold anymore, it travels through my bones, its painful. My chest hurts, my fingers and toes are numb I find the courage, with my heart beating loudly, I was sure she could hear it. I stutter the name "gr gr gra granny can I please climb into bed with you" the answer comes swiftly, angrily, venomously, "NO you are not clean enough to be in my bed" there it is the cold truth, in that moment I know I don't matter to this woman, I am only a pest, a nuisance, a pain and an inconvenience to be dealt with.

I shut down, I learn to endure pain, physical and emotional, to lock it all away, I do it to protect me and to protect the adults in my life. I learn to do it young, and I don't unlearn it until I'm a mature women.

I also learn that the pain my granny holds in her body is deep and wide and all consuming. I don't understand that at this young age, I don't understand it for a few decades, but when I do understand it, it has a profound impact on my life and it's quite shocking how it parallels with my own adulthood.

THE BOLERO

*W*hen I was seven I made my holy communion with my entire class. We all wore white dresses and white veils, and royal blue cloaks, white shoes, white socks, and carried white prayer books. We all looked like angels, we were beautiful, treasured, loved little girls. Our people all showed up to the chapel to see us, and wish us well, among my people were my Mum, and my auntie Delia, some of my big cousins, and my granny M.

My auntie Delia knitted me a white angora bolero with a satin ribbon. I was the only girl in my class to have one. I felt so special, so loved, so treasured. My auntie Delia was my godmother and I adored her. All her children were teenagers and older, she had raised them well. She looked after me often and took great care of me.

I had a lazy eye and had to wear a patch on my good eye, auntie Delia would look out for me because I was blind as a bat with my good eye patched. I almost got knocked over by a car on her street wearing my patch, so she knew she had to watch me like a hawk.

Auntie Delia lived in a lovely home, with a great big room, that's what we called it, the big room, it was only used when we had a party at her house. There was a piano in that room. It was so exciting to us, to sit there and play on that piano. She also had a balcony, we could climb out the window and be on the balcony. It was like magic.

I loved being at auntie Delia's house. I loved my big cousins. Bobby, Mattie, Georgie and Nettie. They all treated me like gold, like a wee treasure. It was the nicest thing to have big older cousins.

So going back to my bolero you can see how much I loved my auntie Delia. I wore my bolero with pride, showing it off, touching its softness, admiring its prettiness, appreciating its warmth. I still have a picture of my first communion and my bolero with the biggest smile on my face. What a day for a little girl to feel like a process or a bride, what an a godmother to make her godchild feel and look a little different than everyone else on that special day. I adored my auntie Delia

THE BRIGHT SUN
OF SUMMER

*I*t was summer like no other, I was eight, with long curly white hair, tanned skin, not burned like usual, and a big smile on my face. We were in Canada (my Mum and me) visiting my big sister Susan, my brother In law Johnny, my nephews Rob and Arthur who were three and one. We were staying for six whole months. It was bliss.

They lived in a house with a front and back door, they had a yard, with grass and trees and a fence. My big sister was beautiful, she had beautiful brown hair and a warm smile, she was trendy and fussy and a bit of a perfectionist. My nephews were adorable and it was like I was a big sister to them.

I loved that summer the sun in my face, the visits to the zoo, my new bathing suit with a skirt attached it was pale yellow and white and I loved it so much. I'd never seen one like that in Scotland, so I thought I was special. My brother in laws family were so good to us, they took us into their hearts and showed us how to see Canada in a big way.

Ann and Walter had a lost a daughter to heart disease, she had a hole in her heart. she would've been the sane age as me. They really spoiled me they were the ones to buy me the bathing suit and take me to the zoo with their other daughter Sherry.

Canada was beautiful to me. I learned how to ride a bike. My Dad wouldn't let me do that in Scotland, but my friend let me ride her brothers bike, first with training wheels and then without. I thought I was flying, the feeling of freedom to go that fast with the wind in my hair, I was in love.

Summer in Canada felt different than summer in Scotland, it was brighter, warmer, sunnier, so much more of everything good and wholesome. I had cousins Pat, John and Yvonne who I would visit and play with. My aunt Ella and uncle Pat lived in the same city. We would see them from time to time. Go there for dinner. Things seemed darker at their house, it was brighter at my big sisters house. They were younger, fresher, more engaged and involved.

I remember upsetting things happening that summer and fall but I choose to shine a light in the bright sun of summer and the sheer joy I felt almost every day. The long nights, the sunsets in the big prairie sky, the kids playing in the neighborhood, my nephews with their little cars and curious questions, their tanned noses and adorable smiles. They were my light, my love, my sun, my moon, my joy, my little people. They were my Canada along with the sun.

A DAY BY THE SEA

*W*e're on the train, heading to Ayr, it's on the sea, and by the race track. I'm with my parents and my best friend Helen. We're the same age, three months apart, she has red hair, in ringlets, I have strawberry blonde hair, in ringlets We are dressed identical. My parents have agreed that we can pretend to be twins, so that when people ask they will go along with it. The train ride is fun, we're in a carriage with some other people. My Dad reads the paper, he calls it (studying form) that means, he's checking out the horse races for the day, and choosing which horses he'll bet on for each race. We aren't supposed to interrupt him, when we do, he becomes irritable, and snaps sharply at us to stop it.

My Mum engages in the game of twins with us, and the other people in the carriage believe we are twins. We play eye spy on the train and my Mum joins in. We read our comic and chat endlessly about seeing the sea. We are two enthralled girls, anticipating a wonderful day.

We finally arrive and we head straight to the race track. There are tons of men at the track. My Dad is dressed in a suit and tie, my Mum in a skirt and jacket, she's wearing heels, and she's just beautiful. My Dad goes to make his first bet, and we wait for him, he returns and tells us the name of his horse, we watch the race, excitedly chanting the name of his horse, Go Joey, Go Joey, Go Joey. The race ends, and my Dad runs off to place his bet on the next race. People all around us start dropping tickets on the ground me and Helen pick them up, we play a game of buying and selling tickets. My Dad comes back and we repeat the process all over again. This goes on for hours, we get tired we want our day by the sea.

We finally leave and go to the beach, we walk along the sand and listen to the waves coming in, we get ice cream cones and happily skip away the day. We're happy to have made it to our happy place, we are enthralled by all we see, hear and feel.

We take the train back to Glasgow, falling asleep on the way home. We wake up and get on a bus to our house. We had a good day, we want to do it again soon. It was fun being twins.

SEBA BEACH

*D*uring our six month stay in Canada when I was eight. We went on a holiday, there were my auntie Ella, her sons Pat and John and daughter Yvonne, my sister Susan my nephews Robbie and Arthur, along with my Mum and I. This was not the typical holiday we generally took back home, so it was very different for my Mum.

Seba Beach is a very small place, we rented a cottage, or a cabin. I think we were a bit crowded, but as kids go, we were fine. It was very hot, and there wasn't a lot for the adults to do, other than care for us children. My Mum couldn't get her medicine (her vodka) as neither my sister nor my aunt drank at this time. So I'm sure she was anxious about that.

As kids we were playing fine. Being the only girl of the older kids I wanted to play house and I wanted Pat to play the dad and John to be the son. John didn't like this idea so he was pouting, Pat and I were both telling him to just play along, but he went in the house and told on us. So my auntie Ella told my Mum that I was being too bossy and that she needed to have a talk with me. The next thing I know is I'm getting pulled off my feet by my pony tail. My Mum is screaming at me that I'm too bossy, that I should just shut my mouth and not say anything at all, as she hits me across the bum, then across the face, because now I'm crying and wailing and she wants me to stop it immediately. My sister is trying to pull my Mum off me, my auntie is trying to talk to my Mum to calm her down it was total mayhem.

It was the worst holiday of my life, but I remember us going back home to Scotland and my Mum telling my dad what a hell hole Seba Beach was, and what she had to endure while she was there. She said she would never go back to another place like Seba Beach again. This story was told for years.

I was always so dumbfounded that she never mentioned that she lost her mind, and beat up her daughter pulling her hair out and dragging her across a room, while shouting at her the entire time.

I will never lose that image in my mind, it was one of pure chaos and sheer terror reigned on a little girl who was just trying to play house.

ROTHESAY

*F*or many years we went to a little place named Rothesay for holidays. Our auntie Martha bought a one bedroom flat there, it held two double beds in the bedroom a double bed in the front room and a pull out single bed. One year we went with my auntie Anna, my cousins, Edana, Frank, Robert, my Granny M along with my Mum and me.

Frank and Robert shared a bed, auntie Anna, my Mum and I shared a bed, and Edana and Granny shared the bed in the front room. We had such a great time. We would go to the beach for most of the day, or play mini golf with my auntie Anna, she was such a cool auntie, she did fun things with us. We would browse the wee shops, and go into arcades, I rented a bike, and accidentally took the paint off a car. Frank told on me and I was grounded from renting a bike again.

In the evenings we'd stroll along the waterfront, or go to a market, or a live play. There were tons of options and fun things to do. We'd chase each other, playing tag, run with the wind in our hair. Get sunburned, but go back out the next day to build more sand castles.

I loved those holidays. We were so close. I was raised as an only child, my only sister being fourteen years older than me, had immigrated to Canada when I was two, so my cousins were like my siblings. Due to being an only child I thrived in being around my cousins. It made me incredibly happy, we had the greatest time together.

My granny M was good to me on that holiday too. Edana was always her favorite, which is why she got to sleep in her bed with her, but it was okay. I was as snug as a bug tucked in between my wee mammy and my lovely auntie Anna.

They were beautiful those two women, both blonde with tiny noses, slim, trim and particularly relaxed on that holiday. I often remember them both being heavy with life burdens, but not on this trip. It's a lovely memory of family time together.

My cousins were really clever, Edana became a stock broker working in London, Hong Kong and New York, Frank became a wonderful teacher, going to an academy, and gaining many accolades. Robert became a famous makeup artist for people like Nicole Kidman and Tom cruise to name a few. Later came Suzelle, who became a hairstylists but is now running her own business. They were all so successful - I on the other hand struggled through school, and came into my own later in life.

I eventually went back to school as an adult and earned my certification in coaching. I worked for a community college as an outreach worker at a jail, teaching anger management skills, life management skills, career development, skills, women's self esteem workshops and parenting classes.

Those women sacrificed so much to raise successful adults and they couldn't have been prouder of us on those holidays to Rothesay or when we walked across a stage with an award in our hands. We came from good stuff.

THE LISMORE TRIP

*W*hen I was twelve I went on holiday with my Aitchison cousins. From oldest to youngest they were: Isobel, Mairi, Jean, Lesley, Willie and me. Morag was not there and that was the reason I was allowed to go. I was so excited for this trip. I loved being around this group of cousins. My uncle Willie drove us up, to Oban where we took the ferry across to the isle of Lismore. My aunt Mairi was the mum of this group of children and she ran a tight ship, she had to, they were a tough bunch as I would find out for myself.

The Isle of Lismore is where my aunt Roma resided with her husband uncle Donald and their three children Morag, Gilleasbuig, and Rachael, They had a small croft with cows, sheep, chickens. They were all so unfarlimiar to me. We seldom went to Lismore, and they came to Glasgow perhaps once a year. So I hoped I would get to know them more on this trip.

Our trip in the car did not go well. I did not travel in cars very often, let alone on windy roads, so I became car sick, which meant we had to stop to clean me and my mess up. I wasn't winning friends with this start to our holiday.

We stayed in the wee White House. It was tiny. Room for beds downstairs and a loft upstairs where Isobel, Mairi and I slept. We had boiled eggs for breakfast, and because I was a boiled egg hater, I seldom ate them. When I did my granny M mashed them up in a cup - they were disgusting! But I had to eat them. My granny N on the other hand would use a sand timer and make a game out of it and cook them till they were hard. She would cut the top off it, and I would eat it with pleasure

So here I was sitting with a large group and I didn't know how to cut the top off my egg. So I spoke up and asked my aunt Mairi to do it for me. Well she couldn't believe her ears, she said "Roma Nelson you're twelve years old and you don't know how to cut the top off your egg" she was not impressed. Everyone looked at me just shocked, even Willie could cut the top off his egg. I was so embarrassed I didn't know where to look, what to do, my face was crimson,- I ran out the door crying, acting like s baby. Not a good start to a holiday. I wanted to fit in so badly, and here I was standing out like a sore thumb.

We eventually got through breakfast, and out we went to explore, we ran the roads and the fields, but my method of running didn't measure up to Isobel and Mairi so they would laugh at me constantly. They would cross the fields, jumping through the barbed wire fences and I would get scratched on my legs. I was a hot mess.

We'd run down the road and I'd fall. Scraping my knees collecting gravel in them I would weep for my Mum, but by the time that holiday ended I had learned to toughen up.

We would wash our hair, then aunt Mairi would take us outside to rinse it with cold well water. I screamed so loud when she did that. She told me "your parents can probably hear you all the way in Glasgow"

We went to calleh which is a dance, and everyone was up doing Scottish dances to a lively band, it was great fun, until the vicar's son kept asking me to dance. I had to say yes, I would've been strongly reprimanded had I refused, but I knew those two Mairi and Isobel were never going to let me live this down.

When we got home to Glasgow, I had knees that were hit by road crush, a massive lump on my head from a bee sting, my hair was stringy, and I was as happy as anyone could be. My Mum took one look at me and asked "what did you do to my lassie?"

We had a blast, they toughened me up, I developed a few new skills, I became a better runner, a good dancer, and I managed to take a joke, so I built a thicker skin.

To this day I still get teased about the egg cutting episode. The last time I was home in 20/9 my cousin Lesley bought me a kitchen gadget which takes the top off an egg. When she handed it to me, we fell about the floor in laughter till the tears ran down our faces. It's a great story to this day.

I fell in love with the wee White House, with my aunt Mairi and all my cousins that year and I really fell in love with the isle of Lismore. It is such a beautiful, lush, green part if the world, with many wee lambs roaming about the green hills. The smell of the sea is incredible as is the view of it.

Every time I go home we visit Lismore, it's such a peaceful place on the planet. I have adored my visits with my aunt Roma, the sharing of stories, and the answering of questions it is the best feeling is arriving on that island, the worst is leaving it. My aunt Roma and uncle Donald have passed away, but Lesley stays very rooted there, and Gilleasbuig, his wife Norma, along with their son Ewan and his wife remain, to keep the family crofting and fishing. I look forward to my next trip.

HEAL THE HIDDEN SCARS

As a five year old I could be described as an anxious child. Some trauma had already happened in my life, so I didn't cope well with new, different or stressful situations. I had a toothache so my Mum took me to the dentist. I don't remember much, except sitting in that big chair, and this old man with white hair and a white bread coming towards me with a mask to put on my face. I freaked out, had a melt down, started crying, hitting with my hands. The next thing I remember is my Mum pulling my arm almost out of the socket as the dentist threw us out of the office. She was screaming at me, that she would never take me to the dentist again, and she never did.

My godmother my auntie Delia took me back to the dentist to have my tooth pulled, I learned to hold all my fears inside, not let them out, just block it all to protect the adults in my life, so everything would be easier for them, and safer for me.

My teeth were in terrible shape, by the time I was fourteen, I decided to take myself to the dentist, I had cavities everywhere, I was embarrassed to smile, to laugh, to let anyone see my teeth. The dentist said my teeth were beyond repair, he advised they all be pulled out and dentures be made to replace them. My Mum finally came with me, as I was to be put out for this procedure.

After the procedure I was shell shocked. I couldn't speak properly, I couldn't eat properly I would look at myself in the mirror and burst into tears. I wouldn't go out or see anyone. My Mum's cousin and his family were living with us, so my cousin decided to take me to a movie. We came back and I felt awful. I don't remember the next days, a dirty instrument had been used in my mouth and I had an infection right through my body. Our family doctor was called out and started administering antibiotics by injection three times a day. I was told I could've died. Our doctor was furious with our dentist and with my parents. What the hell was everyone thinking he wanted to know, allowing s child to go through such a traumatic ordeal. He went so far as to go face to face with the dentist to confront him on such actions.

I spent the next six weeks at home as my gums and body healed. I was terrified when I started to get better. I was fourteen, just getting interested in boys, I had such high anxiety of having to kiss a boy and him being disgusted with my false teeth. I would find myself looking in the mirror when I was alone in the house, I looked different, I hated my smile, it looked nothing like me, I would just weep. One day my Mum's cousins wife came home and found me in tears, she was so kind to me, she had brought me a cake from the bakery. I could only eat soft things, it hurt too much to eat anything hard.

We lived in a high rise building during this time. Word had got out through my parents about what had happened to me. So when I was finally well enough to go back to school I would be greeted every day by the caretakers son who was my age, he would be in the lobby waiting for me and he would chant "your teeth are like stars, they come out at night." I would be totally shattered inside and I'd end up in tears, this went on for weeks. One day I came home and there he was with his smart mouth and his smirky smile and his chanting words and I lost it, I beat him to a pulp, all the anger had turned to rage, and every single bit of that rage was taken out on his body.

Later that night his Dad showed up at our door with his son who had two black eyes, he said to my Mum look what your daughter did to my son, my Mum responded by saying "It's about bloody time she did it, should've come sooner" and slammed the door on their faces.

I believe this experience had a profound impact on me. To this day I have to adjust to trying to eat with false teeth, to getting new ones that don't fit properly. Seeds and nuts are painful to eat, they get caught under my plate

Child neglect has a lasting effect, it impacted my self worth, self esteem, my beliefs and how i see myself in the world. If my parents didn't think I was worthy of time, attention and care, why would anyone else. I made bad choices based on this neglect and other aspects of neglect. It's taken an entire adult life to heal the hidden scars, and forgive the adults who caused them. But I have, and for that I am so grateful, I can now live in peace.

THE SAFE HOUSE

*G*ranny Nelson was my safe place. Her house, her hand, her bosom, her fire, her home. She was a wonderful cook, I ate almost everything she cooked, she made yummy desserts and the best homemade soup in town.

We went to Grammy Nelson's every Sunday for dinner. First in Cranhill where she had a front and back door. I loved that house. It also had a front and back garden. Aunt Molly and uncle John lived with her in the three bedroom house.

There was a big picture window in the living room and I loved to look out it. It had a comfy couch and a chair for uncle John. A dining table and chairs with a bookcase a tv. The kitchen was small, it had a pulley to hang wet clothes on, a bathroom downstairs and three bedrooms upstairs.

Granny wore lipstick, fur coats, and hats, she was posh. She married into a family with a business but my grandfather her husband and his brother lost the business by gambling. He died before I met him, but he was adored by my dad and I'm not sure what the others thought of him.

My granny shopped at Goldberg, it was an expensive department store. Good quality, high priced. If I went with her I had to be dressed properly. Perfectly white socks, clean polished shoes, a nice coat and dress and a hat. It was an adventure going to Goldbergs, they had unique clothes and household items and we were on our best behavior.

My granny was always nice to me. I remember her being nice to all of her grandchildren. We would all laugh with her when we were older and she lived in Shettleston. Or even at the cranhill house. I loved it when my cousins came we had the best time together. Or at least I would think so.

My dad idolized his Mum, he licked his plate clean when she cooked. He engaged in political conversations with her, they always agreed. They kind of adored each other. My Mum would perm my granny's hair and cut it, wash her windows, read the papers, watch movies and get along just fine together.

Granny loved to knit. She took turns knitting for all of her grandchildren. We always got a Christmas present usually a nightgown or a underskirt, maybe some chocolate.

Our granny died when I was sixteen of bowel cancer. I was heartbroken. I fell to pieces the day of her funeral and I didn't go. I regret that decision to this day.

My granny was my safe place. When things got bad with my parents drinking she would take me home with her. She wouldn't dare send me with then. I felt safe in that house, loved in that house, taken care of in that house, seen and heard in that house. I was allowed to be a child in that house, I didn't have to look after adults, they looked after me in that house. When I'd do guided meditations as an adult and they'd say go to a safe place if go to my granny Nelson's. Even as an adult I could still experience that comfort, warmth, tenderness, safety, security, enfolding me, there was nowhere in the world like it.

When my grandchildren come over I try to provide that same environment for them. I always want them to remember Nana's house as a safe, warm, loving, comforting place that enfolds them.

FRIDAY NIGHT

*I*t's Friday after school I'm fifteen, walking home, every fiber in my body is vibrating. I hate Friday nights, it's the start of the weekend and I should be excited. I dread them instead. There is always chaos in my house on the weekend, the drinking starts on Friday night, sometimes Thursday now. It's overwhelming I'm anxious, but I don't understand that word yet, I don't understand that state yet, but that's what I am. The arguing will start in a few hours and it might turn into a fight, a physical fight….

I get home, eat dinner, watch the news, and the drinking begins. I want to go to my friend Trisha's house, but she's busy tonight, so I'm stuck at home. I go in my room, listen to music and read a book. Everything is quiet for now, I try to relax, but it's impossible - it's Friday night, not a night to relax.

I hear their music playing, it gets louder, Nat King Cole is singing, they love him, so do I actually, but I'd never admit it. I hear them getting louder, the argument has begun, I start to pace in my small room, I look out the window, at the skyline from the eleventh floor, I wish I was out there somewhere, anywhere away from here. My breathing is beginning to change. more rapid. My mind is racing, what should I do, where should I go.

They get louder, shouting now, both slurring, I stop breathing, holding my breath, terrified! I hear my Mum shouting my name, over and over again ROMA! ROMA! ROMA! I shake from the top of my head to my baby toes as I walk into the living room. My Dad is standing over my Mum lunging at her, I scream at them to stop. I start to cry, I can't stop shaking and crying, and then I begin to weep. Will this ever end?

My Dad backs off, sits on the couch, lights a cigarette, mumbling to himself. My Mum looks at me, totally unfocused. In this moment I hate them, I hate both of them. I walk back to my bedroom, still crying, I throw myself on the bed, and punch my pillow. I want to die, I want to escape this nightmare called Friday night.

Time passes and then it all starts up again. I can't cope I run out the door. I run to my neighbors, her name is Annie and she's small, tiny, I wake her up. I'm weeping. I beg her to let me in, she does but before she can close the door my Dad rushes in behind me. He tries to grab me, I jump out of his way, he lurches for me, I jump again, he chases me around the couch as Annie screams at him to get out of her house. He finally grabs me, and tiny Annie hits him. He stares at her, shocked. She screams again. GET OUt! He finally leaves.

I vibrate, weep, I shrivel up into a fetal position. Annie comforts me, she puts a blanket around me, she finds me a nightie, she tells me to get undressed, she makes tea while I change in the bathroom. We talk for a while, she lets me sleep in her single bed with her, she tells me it's going to be okay, that he can't get back in.

I finally sleep only to wake up to face Saturday night, and the nightmare will start all over again!

SISTERHOOD

*I*t seems to me that I longed for a sister my entire life. As a child it seemed so far out of reach, my sister lived so far away, in Canada. She was fourteen years older than me so for both those reasons she was a life time away. When I was growing up she would send these incredible gifts from Canada for Christmas.

One year it was a Chatty Cathy doll. She had blonde hair, freckles on her face, she had teeth for her smile, and a Canadian accent when you pulled her string. I already received a Chatty Cathy doll that year, she had short blonde hair, no freckles, no teeth, and no Canadian accent. I adored my Canadian Chatty Cathy. I took her everywhere with me. Showed her off, treasured her, she was softer, more pliable, than my other one and she wore the cutest dress.

One day we were at my granny N's and I left her on the couch, my Mum sat on her, and broke her string. I was so upset. I cried, yelled, wept, I was shattered. I said mean things to my Mum so she slapped me across the face. It was a terrible ordeal. My Chatty Cathy shut down, and so did I.

We went to Canada when I was eight my Mum and I for six months. We stayed with my sister, but it didn't feel like she was my sister. She was married, had children, a job, a busy life, very little time for me. What could we possibly have in common, nothing.

Susan came to Scotland when I was twelve with my niece Denise., we lived in an old tenement building, with no bathtub or shower, my Mum was embarrassed, but Susan made the best of it. Susan took me to see The South Pacific movie, I remember it just being us, and I still wasn't comfortable with her. What did we have in common - nothing!

When I was seventeen we went to Canada for three weeks. Both my parents and myself. I was very shy, timid, awkward, but I fit in well with my nephews and niece. My sister and I talked more now, we visited more and I tried much harder to have things in common.

By the time I was eighteen I had immigrated. My sister lived in a different city than me, I would work all week and take a greyhound bus to visit them every weekend. We were becoming closer, the whole family. It was lovely. I enjoyed my visits very much, looking forward to them all week. I don't think I realized how busy life was for her then, she worked full time, raised three kids, and ran a household with little help from her husband. I sure didn't help much when I showed up on the weekends (I'd do that differently now if I had the chance) on top of me visiting sometimes my parents would come too. That would turn into a drinking fest and I along with my oldest nephew hated it. These episodes often turned into fights.

Eventually my sister and family moved to Edmonton and I loved that. We grew closer, spent many evenings together, spent time at the holidays together. Susan was an amazing cook, she taught me how to prepare many good dishes.

Sadly my sister battled with alcoholism and depression which led to many episodes of stress for her and her family. It resulted in her twenty five year marriage ending which really broke her heart. After some time apart Susan ended up in treatment for her alcohol consumption, where she met her second husband. Due to his work they moved to Ottawa, and once again we were separated by cities.

Every once in awhile Susan and Tom would come to visit her kids and we would get to see them. I would write letters which she kept, My sister was funny, hilariously funny. I would laugh so hard my stomach would hurt. I miss that, I miss her, we never got to be really close, but we got better after a while. We healed some things that were broken between us, and we left some things broken between us. I miss her so much. I miss my people, my Mum, my Dad and my big sister. The four of us once went to an Englebert Humperdinck concert together, it was a birthday gift from our dad to us. I hated it, Susan loved it. I wish we would've done more things just the four of us.

Susan had a hard life, a tough childhood, a lonely road, I understand all that now. I wish she could've opened up more, let her feelings out, but that wasn't her way. She held it all in, and we all lost out due to that silence.

WE ARE FOREIGNERS

There was a tree sitting in the yard, outside the front room window, it was enormous, a weeping Willow, it's leaves hung low, and moved gracefully in the wind. I loved that tree and I loved that home. It was yellow like the sun, a pale yellow, just how I imagined Canada soft, breezy and ever so light. Not heavy or dense or drowning in despair like Britain at the time of Margaret Thatcher. The Iron Lady they called her. She was brutal, dangerous, ruthless, cruel. We had to get away so we came to Canada. Pierre Trudeau with his pirouette, liberal, fun, strong, young, and free. Like Canada he represented freedom, prosperity, opportunity, abundance, and above all hope.

I'm back at the house with the willow tree. It's beautiful inside and out. We are new to this country, my parents and I. We are at my brother in laws, sister's house. Her name is Zed, her husband is Rocky. They are warm, welcoming caring and funny. I enjoy being in their home. Zed has helped me find a job. Everything is new, somewhat overwhelming, we are white, speak English, (but with a Scottish accent-not always easy to understand) We are foreigners but with the best support system one can imagine. So what's the problem? Well for me not much. I'm 18 young, excited, hopeful. For my parents who are in their late 40's early 50's it's more daunting. Work isn't as easy to find at first. We rent a house from my sister and brother in law, but we know nothing about cutting grass, growing flowers, cleaning gutters, caring for a property. We've only ever lived in rented apartments with little maintenance so we fail as renters of a home. Soon we find ourselves renting an apartment as my sister sells her house. We are all relieved.

The first winter is harsh, my parents can't find steady work. I'm the only income earner in our home. I pay all the bills, buy the groceries, buy little bits of furniture when I can. My dad is depressed, angry, lonely, despondent. He feels useless. He breaks into fits of rage at times. Taking it out on my Mum, blaming and shaming her. I can't cope with the outbursts, they overwhelm me, so I run to Zed and Rocky's house. I tell them what's going on, they listen and make me tea. We visit for awhile then Zed drives me home. Things have calmed down for now, until the next time.

My Mum is depressed too, she watches tv day and night, she checks out completely by watching tv, it becomes very lonely in our family, each trying to cope alone, not together at all. I have yet to make friends, it's hard, harder than I could've imagined. I lose my Scottish accent quickly - I'm trying to fit in, not stand out. I don't want to be misunderstood, I don't want to be stared at when I speak, I want to be included, accepted, engaged with, understood.

I finally get invited out by friends at work. We go to a play, it's awkward, they smoke pot, I've never been around anyone who ever smoked pot. They offer me some but I decline, no way I'm trying that stuff. I feel uncomfortable, left out again, one more way I don't fit in, but I have to accept it. I'm not smoking pot. I don't even know what it does to you. It's the unknown to me, the unfamiliar, it's the strangeness of being with new people and trying new things that really terrify me. I want to get past these thoughts and feelings.

I eventually meet friends through work. We go out together, to the ballet, to movies., to lounges and dances. They are nice people. I move in with Terry from work. It feels strange not living at home, being a roommate, having a roommate. It seems to be going well, I'm adapting, adjusting, when suddenly Terry's best friend and previous roommate's parents are killed in a car accident. Terry asks me to move out so her friends can move back in, she had been traveling Europe and suddenly has to come home to face this awful experience. I count my blessings and move home with my parents.

My Mum finds work, my Dad finds work and I keep up with my

job, my new friends, my new country, my visits to see my sister, brother in law and niece and nephews and I settle into a routine of some kind of normalcy. I write letters home, almost daily to my best friend, to my cousins, to my aunts. I am still very homesick, I miss my people, I really miss my people, even today 40 some years later I still miss my people but if I ever decided to go live there again, I would miss my people here, so there is no winning, I will always miss my people.

Today I am grateful that I have a White House, no willow tree, but it feels safe, warm, loving, like the people in it. We became our own version of Zed and Rocky, we laugh a lot in this house, and sometimes we watch movies and cry together my Ian and I, but that's another story, for another day.

DADDY'S LITTLE GIRL

*W*hen I was small, really small my Dad bought me a teddy bear with a music box in its tummy. He was my favorite toy. I called him Teddy and he went everywhere with me. We lived in a neighborhood called the Rottenrow - what a name! We lived on the second or third floor with big bars, which I suppose were meant to be a balcony, but to little kids felt like a jail.

Anyway the kids next door were a rowdy bunch, one of the boys took my teddy one day and threw him off the balcony and he smashed into the ground and into a great big puddle. I wailed, distraught, I screamed for my Mum who went down and got Teddy. He was pretty messed up and he couldn't play music anymore. I was so sad.

I thought my Dad walked on water. I adored him, I hung on his every word. I thought he hung the moon. When we were out and came across a dog, he'd pick me up and carry me. If it was cold out, he'd pick me up and tuck me inside his coat and carry me, when he gave me his attention, he gave me his full attention and he called me his wee doll.

As I got older we would cuddle on the chair together and watch movies, often we would both cry., Sometimes I would sit on the back of his chair and comb his hair, even telling him he had a bald spot. When we would go out as a family I would be in the middle of my parents holding both their hands.

My dad had a gambling problem, he was hooked on the horse races. He would bet on the races all weekend long, he would watch the races on tv and run to the betting club to place his bets for the next race. When all this was going on he was a different person. I couldn't talk to him, he couldn't hear me, If i tried to talk to him he would get mad, and yell at me. So I learned to shut up, stay away from him, only come close when it suited him.

When I was twelve he underwent major surgery for a stomach ulcer. He went to my aunt Roma's to recuperate. When he returned he looked healthy, well, new, and that's when the drinking started. Soon it was drinking and gambling and soon after I didn't recognize him at all.

He was a very angry drunk, he held a lot if resentment towards my Mum and it would come out when they both drank on weekends. Neither of them could be counted on to go to for advice or wisdom. They were simply absent. As the weeks turned into months, and the months turned into years I turned into a shutdown shell of my former self.

The fights on weekends sometimes turned physical with each of them drawing blood. I spent more time out of our home than in it. Things didn't get as out of control if I wasn't there. They each told me how they hated each other, but loved me, it was so confusing and painful. They stayed together out of love for me and hate for each other!!! Why?

Once we arrived in Canada things got worse. More money, more drinking, more drinking, more fighting, no escape with gambling, so more drinking. The physical abuse increased, to the point of my Mum having broken ribs, black eyes, unable to walk. It was a war zone. They went through it drunk and I went through it stone cold sober.

They finally split up when I was twenty eight. I was so relieved. I had come to realize how selfish my Dad had been most of my life. He loved me when he needed me. He loved me when no one else was there, he loved me when he was sober and broke, the rest of the time he was too busy for me, too busy for my kids, too busy for our hard little life we were to carve out for ourselves.

I went home to Scotland to look after my Dad when he became terminally ill with cancer. I was staying for three weeks and I stayed for three months. I had become the parent again, I had become the parent at twelve and I had remained the parent. I was laying on his bed with him, holding him when he died. I'd lost another child, I was a mess, a real mess, it took a long time to heal, losing two children three years apart is horrendous, that's what it felt like to me. Grieving was hard, healing was slow, surviving was insurmountable, thriving has become the gift. I am recovered, wholesome and new. I am blessed.

MUM'S MEDICINE

I don't remember a time in my childhood, adolescence and young adult life when my Mum didn't drink alcohol. It changed her, I loved my Mum, I adored her, she was my everything growing up. She did so many things with me.

I used to spend a week every year with my granny N and one year I wanted to take my doll and pram. My Mum walked all the way from our house with me to my granny's house, which was really far, so I could take my doll and pram with me, stopping often, so I could check in my baby doll. Mum was so patient, she walked slowly, stopped often with me, indulged my need to cover and uncover my dolly.

She was a good Mum she would sing to me, and cuddle me, and hold my hand everywhere we went, she was loving Mum, a proud Mum, a doting Mum. Everything about my Mum changed when she drank, she became loud, aggressive, unhappy, angry. I was afraid of her, I wanted to hide from her, and often did.

My dad didn't drink much when I was young, he had a bad stomach ulcer so he couldn't tolerate alcohol. So my Mum would drink at parties or events. Eventually often just at home without events. During these episodes my Mum would start fights with my Dad. They would get very loud, I would get very scared. By the time I was five or six I would pull my own hair out with both my hands begging them to stop. My Dad would say, "Look what you're doing to Roma" and she'd look at me and stop. It was terrifying.

By the time I was seven or eight she would refer to her vodka as her medicine. She would take me to the off license, or the liquor store to pick up her medicine, and she would buy me chocolate and chips. We would walk hand in hand, or arm in arm as I got bigger.

We would attend a party or a family event and all the adults would take turns singing a song. My Mum would sing this song Daddy's Little Girl. She would sing very loudly, she would make me sit on the floor in front of her, she would hold me so tight she'd choke me as she sang this song. I hated it, and I began to hate her.

As I got older my Mum's drinking became more and more severe. The weekends were a nightmare. She would drink to the point where she couldn't walk, then she would scream my name over and over again until I would get out of bed and get her. I would have to try to walk her down the hall, into her bedroom, get her undressed and put her to bed. It was horrendous! I HATED IT! Sometimes I would go to bed and weep.

My Mum drank until I was around thirty years old. She stopped drinking after attending a week long treatment program with my sister. She was with all the family members of alcoholics. It was there that she realized "she was an alcoholic" She told a counsellor there that she was an alcoholic. She came straight to my house when she got out and told me her realization. She apologized for everything she'd put me through and unlike every other apology I'd ever heard this was sincere, it was from the heart, but informed from the head.

I got my Mum back for nine years before she died. I was grateful, ever so grateful. She helped me so much to raise my kids. As a single parent I don't know what I would've done without her for those nine years. We healed what was broken, we built what was lacking and we treasured each other till her last breath. I was with my Mum when she died, I held her hand while she took her last breath and my best friend Debbie held my other hand. It was the hardest most horrendous thing I'd ever done, but to this day I'm so grateful I was with her as she parted this world. I grieved deeply after my Mum died, in so many ways it was like I had lost a child, I had parented my Mum since I was twelve years old. We had reversed roles, even in her sobriety I was still the parent, emotionally. My grief was deep, it took many years to subside. But that's another story.

MY WORST NIGHTMARE

*T*hree weeks after I was married at twenty one we went to a club, we ran into a bunch of Bob's friends from a town in Manitoba and it became a great big party. These guys hadn't seen each other in years so they were catching up on the good old days and having lots of fun and good humor doing it.

We left the club and went to a house party afterwards. I was sitting on a table with my friend Alice, her brother Louie, my friend Brenda and my husband Bob. Different guys from this group would stop by and talk someone would move someone would sit down.

We stayed for about an hour and left to go home. Louie came with us to crash on our couch. We got home and got into bed when Bob started accusing me of flirting with one of the guys who sat beside me for a minute, I completely denied it, all I did was answer his questions, plain and simple. But the next thing I knew he punched me in the face, my head swung back and hit the headboard and I saw stars. I was terrified. I slowly got my bearings as I was weeping, grabbed a blanket and went and slept on the floor by Louie. If Bob was going to try that again there would be someone there to see.

I didn't leave the next day. I was too ashamed to call defeat, instead i allowed other kinds of abuse to take place in that marriage. It was a disaster of a marriage but I couldn't find the strength to leave.

The second time he hit me was when I was pregnant with Jason our oldest son. He was making fun of my false teeth in front of a group of people II had once told him the story of the caretakers son and how he'd chant "your teeth are like stars they come out at night" so here he was a grown man chanting that and laughing at me. I became very distraught and yelled at him to stop the next thing I knew he slapped me across the face in front of all those people. He was cruel and violent, it was my worst nightmare.

I left him the first time when Jason was nine months old. Shortly after I left him I found out he came onto one of Brenda's friends, while I was in hospital with his baby. I went back six more times before I left for good. But that's another story!

Just remember a man only has to hurt us one time for us to get the message that it can happen again.

BROKEN IN TWO

*T*here was a slam of the door, I jumped, scared, what's happening I thought and then another, a different door, but banged open with a foot. I stood up, alarmed. He was yelling at me GET OUT! GET OUT! I stumbled, almost fell, ran to the bedroom to grab my things, my sons things. I threw them in a suitcase as fast as I could as I was weeping,

I had been staying with friends in Scotland, my husband had loused up yet another great opportunity with a fantastic job. We were to settle in Nottingham England but it all fell through. He flew back to Canada to save money for our flights. Me, our two year old son, and our baby in my tummy. We had overstayed our welcome. My poor friend didn't have the heart to tell us to leave so it took her husband kicking us out for it to end. He was tired of not having his home to themselves. Who could blame him? We had been there far too long, my friend had been so gracious, so kind, so patient, so thoughtful - but enough was enough, every good intention has a timeline and we had crossed ours weeks ago.

I left with my son, my baby in my tummy, my suitcase, my stroller for Jason, and not a clue what to do. I had a couple of pounds on me so I went to a pay phone and phoned my dad. He was living with my aunt and her husband I told him what had happened and asked if I could stay there, he said NO very angrily!

I hung up the phone broken in two. Here I was with two babies and homeless how was I going to survive? I grab the suitcase and the stroller and walk for a bit, terrified, my mind is racing, my heart is pounding, my tears are flowing, I have to figure out what to do. I know nothing of homeless shelters, or women's shelters, I know nothing of being homeless so I pace and pray and pace and pray. I decide to call my cousin Georgie I tell her what's happened, I tell her what my Dad said, she tells me to come over. I don't have enough money to get there. I can't tell her this too.

I hang up and walk a few blocks to my mom's cousins house. I tell her my terrible tale, she can see what a mess I am. She gives me money to get to Georgie and Ronnie's I am so grateful.

We arrive there at night, bedtime for my son, I bathe him and tuck him in. My cousin doubled her girls up in one bed so we can have the other single bed. I am so grateful, immensely grateful yet very depressed.

How is this my life? How do my babies deserve this? They are innocent, beautiful souls, how did I get here? How do I get out of here?

My Dad had to help pay for my ticket back to Canada and he was furious about it. Listening to him rant and rave was horrible, I was filled with guilt and shame, but I couldn't stay there I had to leave, I had to return to Canada and try to make my marriage work. It was an utter mess though.

After Jevon was born I'd wake up every day to Bob saying "you better be out of here with those kids by the time I get home from work" I didn't know how to make that happen. It was daunting to say the least, demoralized daily to hear your husband say those words to you. He'd apologize every day, but what could it all mean?

I kept at it until Jevon was ten months then I left. One day he came home and we were gone just like he'd demanded every day. He didn't seem upset at all, very happy actually. That eventually changed. It was a bloody roller coaster, a terrible ride for all of us. It did end, but not until there was one more baby boy and one strong, determined women walking towards the light.

MY BEAUTIFUL BOYS

*I*t happens without us noticing, I blinked and my babies were men. I have three sons, they are named in order of birth Jason, Jevon and Joshua, they are my pride and joy. They were adorable littke boys, who kept me on my toes as a single parent. I left their Dad when I was pregnant with Joshua. Jason was four and it was the day before Jevon's second birthday.,

We were a team the four of us, we faced some major hardships through my pregnancy and beyond, but we always managed one way or another to land on our feet.

I went to a women's shelter when I left for good. It was daunting, but I couldn't run back to my parents again, I needed to face the truth head on and make the decision to really get on with my life. The staff at the shelter were wonderful to me. I had to make a decision about where I was going to live and I was terrified to live in low income housing, so initially we moved into a two bedroom apartment while we went on a waiting list for a unit in low income housing.

We got into the unit of social housing a couple of weeks before Joshua was born. My friends Debbie and Louie helped me clean it, and prepare it for the arrival of a new baby. During my pregnancy I attended a group once a week with other women from the shelter who had left their spouses and partners. They were amazingly kind to me. They had a baby shower for me, providing such necessary items, and clothing.

Once Joshua was born we settled into a routine. It was not an easy life for my babies, but we tried to make the most of it. For the next five years I went for counseling, took some courses at college for upgrading then onto university. I found a program to become a Life Management Skills Coach. I went through the process of applying and enrolling in the program. I managed to get us off social assistance and out of social housing.

My sons had some learning disabilities which required some special attention and schooling. At one point we were involved with six different agencies trying to manage all our needs and issues. We developed a very structured routine. Dinner, make lunches, homework, night snack and bed. It was daunting, but doable.

All three of my sons were athletic, they loved playing hockey, they played hockey day in and day out. They all wanted to play ice hockey, but I couldn't manage it financially I had no idea how to maneuver programs that helped single parents so they never got to play ice hockey. Instead I found a ball hockey league and they played every Saturday. We would take a taxi to and from the location and we would stay most of the day depending on what teams they were on and what time their games were. The kids loved it, they were passionate about it, dug deep and became very good at it. As grown men they still play when they can.

Eventually I got a job working for a local college. I was hired as a coach in a an outreach program working at a jail in a near by community. I finally had benefits and a better salary. We were a bit more stable financially. Prior to this I worked for a non profit organization the pay was low but the rewards were high. I loved that job it fit me like a glove and I thrived at it, but I had kids to think of, and I needed more money to support them.

My boys were my sun and my moon they were the reason I got up in the morning, and the reason I went to work in a jail every day. They were getting older, bigger, eating more, wanting more, and although I did my best I know they didn't have what their friends had, two stable parents who lived together, and trendy clothes and shoes.

Eventually my two oldest sons went to live with their Dad, I was devastated. I felt completely destroying Inside. One of the guys I worked with gave me a book about how boys need their same sex parent and all that relationship can provide. It calmed me right down, I let them go with my blessing. I am so grateful they had the opportunity to do that. Just a couple of years later when Jevon had just turned seventeen Joshua fourteen and Jason nineteen their died died from an overdose of pills on December 23rd 1998. It was devastating, earth shattering, terrifying, numbing, unbelievable.

It was a very rocky few years for us after that. We all battled depression. I had just lost my dad on Easter Sunday that same year and my Mum three years before that. I was walking, breathing, but barely functioning. It took some very intense therapy through s program at the university hospital to start to put me back together. My poor sons had a parent who was dead and a parent who was absent, by mental illness. My heart still breaks when I think of what they had to endure.

It took a lot of hard work to get my boys to men, and that hard work was their doing. I can say I'm a great Mum today because I never gave up, but there were times when my boys needed a great Mum and didn't have one. It is my greatest sadness and my biggest regret that they had to suffer a minute in life let alone a day, a week, a month or a year because of me or the choices I made.

It has been hard to write this piece. I love my boys with all my heart, they will always be my boys, my beautiful boys, who deserve the sun, the moon and the stars. They fight hard to look after their families, whether that be their children and wives, or each other and Ian and I. They have pure hearts, they are good people, with generous dispositions. They make me so proud I am a lucky mama bear.

SPECIAL BOND

When I was home in 1998 looking after my Dad while he was dying from cancer, I had this incredible opportunity to get to know my aunt Mairi. I had always held her in the highest regard. as she was a women who raised seven children mostly single handedly. My uncle Willie, her husband worked away a lot, they had six girls and one boy.

My aunt ran a tight ship, she had to. All her children grew up to be very successful adults, and she was very proud of all of them. Aunt Mairi was very structured, she needed to be. Each of her children thrived in school and in life.

Every morning my aunt would come to visit my dad and I. As my dad became progressively worse, aunt Mairi and I would visit. I would ask lots of questions, and I started to understand how much she disrespected my Dad.

It turned out that my Dad was very spoiled growing up, even right into adulthood. My aunt was fiercely independent, self reliant, and extremely determined. When I was a younger women she thought I was very spoiled, (which I was in some ways) she could see how my parents weren't doing me any favors but she could now see how much I had changed, and how I had become a strong women too.

We talked about so many things, family things, life things, I received great wisdom and advise from my aunt, and I deeply wished I had known her this much my whole life. Aunt Mairi talked to me about losing her parents and how hard it was for her, how after her Mum died she found herself taking the bus to her house just to look at her window.

My aunt Mairi was an inspiration to me, a rock when I needed one the most, an ear when I needed to vent, a companion at the death bed of my Dad, and a loving caring aunt. I was and still am extremely grateful I managed to have so much one on one time with her. She was the icing on the cake, during a very dark experience. I think of her often and to this day I carry a £20.00 note in my purse, because she told me to. She was a remarkable women - I loved her deeply and dearly and I still miss her

Some women just rise to whatever they are called to do, my aunt did that and more with such incredible strength and focus. What a role model, what a women, what a heroine. What an aunt.

FOUR DECADES OF
FRIENDSHIP

*W*e met while working together in the payroll department. I was twenty four and Debbie was twenty five. We got each other right from the start, we had the same sense of humor, and got each other's sarcasm. She was my supervisor, but we gradually became friends., I was married, had a nine month old boy, Debbie was living with her partner Pat. We both lived close to work, and close to each other.

Neither of us lasted at that job for more than a year or so after I started there. I moved back to Scotland for nine months, came back and picked up where we left off. Debbie broke up with Pat, moved and once again we lived close to each other. I was still married now with two children.

I went through a few break ups and reunions with my husband, Debbie was my go to person. I would bare my heart and soul to her, she would do the same with me. Debbie did so well career wise, did well financially, but sometimes struggled with men. We were each other's soft place to fall.

Eventually I left Bob for good. Debbie was my rock. She would spend endless hours playing cards with me or Yahtzee during my pregnancy with my youngest son. I cried more during that pregnancy than ever before in my life, my friend stood by me, comforted me, and sometimes even fed me.

At one point Debbie became pregnant. We were so excited, she wanted a baby so badly. We talked about little else, she went for a very routine ultra sound and was told the baby had no heartbeat. I will never forget that call. I picked her up from the hospital and drove her to her sister's house. We bawled the whole way. They had sent her to the hospital for a D & C which was devastating.

Debbie met Tony and fell in love, getting engaged within a year and then married. I stood up with her on her big day, and watched her life take off in the direction she had longed for.

On the night my Mum died Debbie was with us. There had been various people up visiting that night. Every once in awhile my Mum would ask who was there then she'd go back to sleep. When I told her Debbie was there, she decided to take off her oxygen mask, it was the only thing keeping her alive. We begged and pleaded with her to put it back on to no avail. Eventually I had to accept this is what my Mum was doing, so I sat down and held her hand, and Debbie held my other hand as we wept our faces off. My Mum was trying to decide who she wanted to be there for me - she chose Debbie, she knew she was the one to get me through that awful experience.

I met Ian in 2002 and married him in 2003 Debbie was my maid of honor. She was my eternal side kick, she still is. I treasure this women. I treasure all we've been through together, and separately. She knows things about me that no one else will ever know.

We have been friends for over four decades now. We need to celebrate that. Not everyone has that kind of long term friend. We've had our ups and downs, but we've struggled, fought worked our way through them. I treasure friendship with women, I value this one as near and dear to my heart it is as unique as Debbie is

IN OUR DARKEST HOUR

When my kids lost their Dad to an overdose of drugs it was December 23rd 1998. We woke that morning to Josh asking me what's wrong with his Dad. I didn't know, We had slept over at Bob's because we were going Christmas shopping for our sons, I had slept on the couch. I went upstairs and touched Bob he was cold, freezing cold. I told Josh to get his brothers up, I called 911.

The ensuing minutes were of the shape of sheer terror. The person on the phone was instructing us to get Bob off the bed and onto the floor. Jason had his feet I had his head, and I dropped him. I became a bit hysterical at that point. The rest is a blur until the paramedics arrived. They chased us out of the bedroom, while some asked to see his medication, they asked questions and carried Bob out on a stretcher. They took our boys and me in another ambulance to the hospital.

They put us in a quiet room by ourselves at the hospital, and the doctor came in to tell us Bob had died. We all sat there in shock, tears started to run down my face and the doctor wiped them away with his hand. They sent for the social worker or the chaplin. I remember we went in to see Bob and I let out a blood curdling scream, a wail, the kind you only ever hear in the movies. I know we talked to some people. I don't remember what was said. We finally had to go home. We had no ride, no money, we had left the house with nothing but each other. I called my friend Mary, I told her what had happened and asked her to come get us, but she couldn't. I phoned my friend Susan and told her the same thing she came right away. Susan stayed with us until my friend Patty could get there.

That evening Bob's friends came by, some of my friends like Debbie stopped in, we were a mess. Patty and her daughter Sara spent the night, they changed their Christmas plans and stayed with us until Carol could come. When Carol got there she got busy taking care of us in whatever way we she could.

My friends Cathy, Donna, Gayle and Brenda came and cleaned Bob's house they bought food and prepared a lunch for after the funeral., They stood in the background never expecting accolades but they were so kind.

All my friends and Bob's friends gathered to surround us in love and support. Then the funeral was over and people had to return to their own lives. Carol, Susan, Brenda stayed close. Debbie moved to Calgary. Everyone else, all but disappeared. A couple of months after Bob died the friend that Bob was renting from asked us to leave. My boys were devastated. I did everything but get on my knees and beg her to let us stay, but the answer was no. Shortly after my car was repossessed, and weeks after that my contract with my job was revoked.

I ended up at the university hospital where I was assessed. I had people come see me three times a day at home. I was incredibly depressed, barely breathing. I was eventually admitted into an eighteen week day treatment program. It was intense, harsh, cold, uncaring treatment model. They were hands off therapists and didn't show compassion, caring, or warmth. It was so tough, but I got through it.

I slowly very slowly tried to build a life for my kids again. I started out making $10.00 an hour again. I worked three jobs to try to pay the bills and keep food on the table.

Friends helped where they could. Especially Collette and Ron, who would visit, talk to the kids, and try to keep me going. Also Carol, Susan and Brenda.

I gradually started to gain some inner strength and courage, and managed to feel my feet under me again. My heart still breaks for my sons who went through such hell. It was the saddest, darkest part of their lives, and my precious sons should never ever have had to experience any of it, let alone all if it.

Losing their Dad set them back immensely. To this day it still has an impact on them, they still go through periods of grief, with immense sadness and longing to just have their Dad with them for one more day, one more talk, one more hug, just one more…..of everything, especially to meet their precious, beautiful babies.

They are amazing men, they put so much effort into their lives, their children's lives, along with trying to work and make money to provide for their families. It has been a tough journey for them, but they make me so proud, every single day that they get up and put one foot in front of the other. Debbie and Carol are still strong supporters of theirs, they still show up for big and small events, and they offer quiet support to all three of them. They are the aunts they really needed, the aunts who truly love them. I am eternally grateful for them and to them.

KINDNESS

*I*t was closing in on winter and things were tough with us. Trying to keep a household afloat on very little money was taking a toll everything finally came crashing down. I was in a terrible state, the heat had been turned off and I couldn't pay our rent.

We were huddled in the living room floor sleeping trying to stay warm from the heat from the fireplace. I can't remember who phoned who, if I called Annette or If she phoned me, but I told her the state we were in, and she wired money, it was a lot of money. Over $800.00 my heat bill got away from me.

During this period of time my aunt Mairi and uncle Willie also helped me out, as did my cousin Willie at one point. I was working one job at $10.00 an hour I just couldn't t make it, I was always behind in bills, borrowing from Peter to pay Paul. Things had to change, I couldn't keep asking people to bail me out, it was humiliating, I found extra work at a department store a couple of nights a week and a Saturday, and became a weight watchers leader one night a week. They all only paid $10.00 an hour but with the extra hours things got a little better.

There were many other people in my life who showed me great compassion and kindness during that time of my life, they were good people. Debbie, Carol, Alice and Gully, Louie, Debbie H, Brenda, and my friend Susan. I don't know where my kids and I would've been without the generosity of people who loved us, and who wanted to see us succeed.

This dark period was after I lost my career with the college, after I lost my car, after we lost the house we had been living in, after my kids lost their Dad. We gradually climbed out of that dark place, I eventually got better jobs with more money, met Ian and our lives improved.

I just want to say thank you to all the people who stepped up at the most desperate time in our lives, to shed some light, some heat, some warmth, some hope back into our hearts and souls. Who gave us a hand up so we could get up on our own again and who never ever threw it in our faces, or made us feel terrible. For all of that I am truly truly grateful.

GEORGIE

$\mathcal{G}$eorgie is my older cousin, ever since I can remember I have loved Georgie. She took me under her wing when I was little and I have stuck to her like glue. I would go on dates with her and her now husband Ronnie, getting right in the middle of them -I'm sure they just loved that! I spent tons of time in their home and I would follow her around, making a pest of myself.

Georgie is eleven years older than me, we can be totally honest and real with each other. She is funny, so funny, we have spent much of our time together laughing. Her quick wit and ability to laugh at herself is so refreshing to be around.

As I got older I would baby sit her girls Yvonne and Sharon we would go on vacations together Georgie and Ronnie with the kids and my friend Janice.

We went to Scarborough one year, where we took turns going out and staying home with the kids. They were good to us Georgie and Ronnie. I loved being around them.

My auntie Delid, Georgie's Mum bought a convenience store Georgie would work in there at night, and I'd go visit her. I often slept at her house on weekends. I followed her everywhere, even as a teenager.

Georgie was like a big sister to me, she still is. She has always been that person who I can take my troubles to, and get soothed, nurtured and given advise, on what my next steps were to be,

Georgie and Ronnie came out to Canada for Jason's wedding in 2012.

I was delighted when they said they were coming we had a fantastic couple of weeks together. I loved having them here. We took them to the mountains, to Jasper and Canmore. They were astonished with how beautiful this country was. It was such a privilege having them at tge wedding and showing them another part of Canada. We stayed in little cabins by the river and Ronnie said he finally felt like he was in Canada.

When I go home I feel at peace In their home Itd my home away from home. They are delightful to be around, good natured, great company and Donnie is a fantastic cook. It's the most delicious meals he serves.

I was an annoyance when I was wee, a curious teenager in my youth, an inquisitive young adult, and a troubled young women at times in my life. Georgie saw me through every stage and was never afraid to tell me to smarten up if I was heading in the wrong direction.

We see each other every time I'm home, we text or phone often. or face time. We can pick up where we left off the last time we talked. It's like no time has passed at all. That's a blessing, a luxury and a great comfort to me bring so far away. My roots are solid as my family loves me and I feel it thousands of miles away.,

Georgie is a good kind, funny, engaging, thoughtful, dedicated human being. She dotes on her family and their pets she is a wonderful sister, Mum, gran, aunt, sister, wife, cousin and friend. I don't know who I would laugh so much with, or tell my woes to, if I didn't have oor Georgie. She is a bright light in my life.

ONE TRUE LOVE

$\mathcal{W}$e met for coffee on a Saturday afternoon. It was half a block from home on a blind date. My supervisor at work got this going. We had communicated a few times by email and he'd sent me a Robbie Burns poem on Burn's Day. His name was Ian MacKinnon, could it be any more Scottish?

We visited for a couple of hours over tea and coffee and I found myself laughing a great deal, he was easy to be around, easy to talk to and easy on the eyes. He had red hair and blue eyes, and a warm smile.

We went our separate ways, deciding we'd get together again. He phoned the next day. The 2002 Olympics were on and he was just about to watch a game. We agreed to talk again soon. He invited me over for dinner, we had a lovely evening. It ended up we only lived a block from each other. Ian walked me home, he gave me a little kiss on the check and watched me get inside the house. I was in awe.

I began to go over every night for dinner as he was on a lay off from work. My oldest two boys had already moved out, and my youngest one spent most of his nights with them, so I started to spend some nights there too. Josh wasn't ready to be on his own so we decided to get a place together and Josh came with us.

On my birthday we got engaged, and the following July we got married. We had a very simple wedding with family, friends and lots of kids. We were piped out of the church by my supervisors daughter and later in the evening we had a piper and dances come and perform for us.

I was in love, in harmony, in sync, in peace, in contentment. We had very little when we got together, we had no car, we rented a townhouse, with bits and pieces of furniture, but we made a cozy and peaceful home, and we loved it.

We agreed on politics, on world affairs, on moral and social issues. We were a team. We came into our marriage with a big debt from a charge that Ian had incurred and we had to pay over $37K back to the government of Alberta. Neither of us were making great money, but we made our monthly payments every month. Ian's Dad sold us a car and let us make payments on it. So now we had a way to get around.

Ian's Dad eventually gave us money for a down payment in our house which we were so grateful for. We have been so fortunate.

I gained a family with a sister and brothers and Ian gained sons and grandchildren it has been a win win. We love each other deeply, we care about our families immensely. We almost always don't like the same people for the same reasons. We have embraced each other's friends.

This past year we both retired, we are finding our way, we've taken our young grandchildren on vacation to Drumheller, we went out to Victoria for two weeks, we are heading to Canmore in a couple of weeks. I am unbelievably happy that I met my love, that I get to spend my life with my Ian. That I have the softest most loving place to fall, and the sweetest most human to catch me. This part of my life has been good, ever so good. I am one lucky women, who was born in Scotland, but had to marry a Canadian to get a Scottish name. We are #clanmackinnon

PURPLE HEATHER

My sister in law is named Heather. She is beautiful. She looks at least a decade if not two decades younger than what she is. Heather has long blonde hair, blue eyes a warm smile, a petite body, and a strong spirit.

I came into the family over two decades ago. We have become close. We talk weekly, updates about life, work, kids, vacation plans, health and issues.

We've managed to get a few little mini vacations together on Vancouver island. My happy place, and Heather's home. I love going out there. I love getting to spend time with Heather and my brother in law Dave, along with my nieces and nephew.

We have long talks about all life's ups and downs, play cards, or other games, eat delicious meals as Heather and Dave are incredible cooks. There isn't much that goes on in my life where I don't think "I wonder what Heather will think of that"

We disagree sometimes, but that's okay, we're family and we can do that, it's part of the package. Heather and Dave travel way more than us, sometimes I feel so envious, wishing I could afford to travel like that, but I can't, that's a reality, so I adjust and go from envy to acceptance within a reasonable timeframe Envy only hurts me anyway, it doesn't hurt anyone else.

Heather is very generous, she is an incredible Mom a patient, calm, logical, problem solver. She weighs things out carefully and thoughtfully. I would learn more from being more practical and less spontaneous.

I feel so fortunate to have married into this family, to be related to these amazing people. To have created many fond, touching, fun memories. To be welcomed so often into their home, even when I was a loud, nasty, greedy drunk. I have carried much shame about that and a ton of regret. I have made amends, but sometimes amends don't feel like enough. I still wish I would've behaved with more Grace, would've shown more thoughtfulness and been more generous. My ugly was incredibly ugly when I drank and Heather suffered dearly from my awful selfish, careless behavior.

It's my greatest hope that Heather knows that I think she's worth her weight in good, that she's someone I greatly admire, and finally someone I aspire to be.

The flower heather grows purple in Scotland it is beautiful, magnificent, glorious, breathtaking. Our Heather is the same, she is all the above and more, as she stands in all her glory.

THE BEST GIFTS EVER

Next to having my children and meeting my husband Ian my best gift ever was having my cousins Mairi and Lesley fly in from Scotland to surprise me for my wedding. Their Dad my uncle Willie paid for them to fly to Canada for my big day. It was the biggest surprise of my life and the biggest gift I could ever imagined.

Ian and I went to pick up our wedding rings the Wednesday before our wedding. We were invited to our friends Debbie and Mike's for dinner. Mike picked us up from the mall and took us back to their place. They offered us a drink and we visited a bit. Then they told us they had a surprise for us. They had us stand up, turn around and close our eyes. Then they instructed us to open them. Standing there in front of us, in all their glory were Mairi and Lesley. I threw myself at them. I screamed, I cried, I screamed some more and I cried some more. My heart was pounding out of my chest, my face was beaming, I was sweating, I couldn't let them go. I could not believe they were standing there in front of me.

After we all settled down, they explained that they had communicated with Debbie and she had picked them up from the airport, helped them find a hotel, got them settled. They explained their Dad sent them to represent the family.

They brought gifts, lovely teacups with Scottish sayings on them, a beautiful photo album made by Isobel, a friendship cup, a treasured gift was a broach from their Mum my aunt Mairi who had passed away. It had a thistle on it which is the flower of Scotland. I have that broach still I treasure it. No one ever gave me anything so meaningful as that I proudly wore it on my wedding day.

I loved my wedding day. I love my Ian with every part of my being, he's such a good man, who truly treasures me. We had all his family with us, my three sons, my daughter in law Amanda and my two month old granddaughter Emily, along with my Scottish cousins, and my sister and family.

I had a grateful heart, a joyous soul, a content body, a blissful mind. I had married my best friend, my favorite person, my greatest companion, my lover, my daily laughing pal. I had married my love and I only feel these things deeper today.

FRIENDSHIP

My friend Carol is s treasure to me. She came into my life thirty four years ago, and has remained ever since. We have journeyed through many storms in each other's lives. Carol is funny, light hearted, warn, caring, she smiles easily and talks with strangers often. When Carol cares about a person, she cares deeply. She is a wife, mother of three and grandmother of three. She is an amazing Mom and grandmother. Most of her time is spent helping raise her grandchildren, her dedication and commitment are admirable and enviable.

Carol and I do arts things together, we go to the ballet, candlelight music events, Jann Arden concerts and talks. Jesus Christ superstar plays. We do crazy things like making creative collection boards. She is good at creating, I am not, but that's okay. We cheer each other on.

During some of the darkest days of my life Carol has shown up to guide us through the process. She irons shirts for funerals and makes soup, she holds me while I weep and talks to my sons in their darkest hours. She took oldest my son to live with her for six months, and allowed him to heal, and be a kid after his Dad died. She is the most amazing friend anyone would want in their corner.

We've gone to physics together to have readings done, and had runaway nights off, sharing a hotel room to catch up with each other We a few days away in Canmore where we celebrated her sixty fifth birthday.

We browse and shop and walk, take selfies, laugh and talk, eat and enjoy each other's company.

I couldn't imagine life without this women by my side. She is a true believer in me and I in her. We can be real and stupid with each other. We are blessed.

ROSEMARY'S GRANDDAUGHTER'S

*M*y real name is Rosemary but I've always been called Roma. The Ro from the Rose the Ma from the Mary. I was named after my aunt Roma who also was named Rosemary. I hated my name as a child, also as a young adult. People get it wrong all the time. Wilma, Rona, Rhonda, and on and on it goes. So sometimes I would just tell people my name was Rosemary it was easier, but it didn't seem like me.

There was a song when I was a teenager named Love Grows Where My Rosemary Goes, I loved that song, I loved that my name was in it, and that love could grow where I went. I think that's a special kind of song, and a special kind of thought. I hope it's true.

There is another song with my name it's called You are Rosemary's granddaughter I have three granddaughters and two of them have my name Rosemary as their middle name. I feel so honored that their parents did that. As I get older, I think it's such a beautiful name, I spent most if my life hating it, but I love it now.

I have a friend Mary from Newfoundland she has always called me Rosemary, never Roma, I love how she pronounces my name, she almost sings it, Rose Mary, it sounds so beautiful coming off her tongue.

Imagine writing a story about your name, but I just did. It's for you Amy Rosemary, and for you Jai Rosemary, you are Rosemary's granddaughters, so are you Emily Elizabeth, we danced to this song when you were little, we danced with you in my arms, none of you will remember that, but I'll never forget.

DAUGHTER IN LAW

I've wanted a daughter my whole life, someone to do things with, like shop and chat, decorate the tree, build a bond with, listen to, and talk to. Amanda came into our lives when she was nineteen, she was dating Jason and they were a good match. Amanda was quiet, thoughtful, petite. She would come over with Jason and I'd slowly get to know her.

Later that year Amanda became pregnant with Emily, and at twenty she became a Mom. She was patient, loving, encouraging and tender. Amanda was good with us, and it was so nice to have a girl in the family, well two now including Emily.

As the years went on, we would spend time together at our house or at Jason and Amanda's eventually another baby was on her way another little girl named Amy.

With a complete family of four, we saw lots of them until they moved to a small town. Amanda had found her Dad and was reunited with him, they moved to where he lived and enjoyed getting to know him. The girls loved living out there with horses and plenty or room to roam. They had dogs and cats some ducks at one point. We would enjoy visits to their home and time spent playing games or just visiting.

Jason and Amanda got married in August of 2012. It was a lovely wedding. Amanda was a beautiful bride, she looked stunning, I was so happy to see them together looking so happy,

Amanda is strong, determined, creative, hardworking, passionate about her girls and always willing to try to learn new things. I love seeing her thrive and try new things, go out of her comfort zone and push herself. She has raised one very confident individual in Emily who has clear boundaries and some determined goals. Amy is still in high school and Is still finding her way, but leaning towards photography at the moment. She loves animals, her horses, and country everything.

It is a joy to share dreams with this women Amanda and to be a part of her life, to encourage her as she encourages me. What a blessing it is to have a daughter.

HEART AND SOUL

*G*ranny Milligan was tough in a way that people, who have lived challenging lives are tough. Her name was Susie and she married Robert, together they birthed eight children, two of which they lost. They raised six, Delia, Lizzie, Robert, Ella, Anna and John. They lived in a small room and kitchen. The kitchen consisted of a couch, chair, a kitchen cabinet a side board, a grandmother clock, a table and chairs that gleaned to a shine, a fireplace, a wall mirror. A kitchen sink, a window, and a bed in the recess. It was immaculate. She was a perfectionist. Her children were scrubbed clean every day, they shone like bright pennies. The room had a double bed a dresser, a wardrobe and a window. The window faced the front street, my granny spent hours upon hours looking out that window.

It was a life filled with singing, cooking, bathing, and working. My Mum would tell me stories of how they would all sing on Sunday's while they got bathed, and when their parents cooked. They were good memories. They didn't have much, but they had each other and the valued that.

They would all crawl into bed squeaky clean, together, fighting on who should have to sleep on the outside, they were scared to be on the outside. The older ones usually ended up on the outside

As they got older, they got married, my Mum eloped married a man in the armed forces. Tommy McLaughlin, together they had my sister Susan, they adored her. Tommy was away a lot, my Mum lived in the same building as her parents, but shortly after Susan was born my grandad died from a massive heart attack at work. My granny still had two children at home to raise, with no skill set to work to achieve a living.

Things were very harsh, no pensions were handed out at that time and my aunt and uncle had to find ways to find food for themselves and my granny. Things were tremendously challenging, on top of this they were all grieving. Pulling together to try to help each other and raise the new babies from the older siblings.

As the rest of us grandchildren came along we spent lots of time at our granny's. I went there every day to and from school, I went there for lunch and after school I'd go to her house to purchase her daily groceries. I would do a weekly run too. I attribute my good memory to my granny as I wasn't permitted to write anything down. I had to remember everything by heart. I got really good at it. Granny could t read or write, but I only found this out very recently, that was one reason we weren't allowed to write things down.

Every Saturday I'd get my pocket money for running errands all week I'd get my money and a butter sandwich. She made the best butter sandwiches. I wouldn't eat them from anyone other than granny Milligan.

On the Thursday before my granny died, she sent me for her daily groceries. When I came back my older cousin Mattie was there, she loved Mattie so much, granny gave me my pocket money, my butter sandwich and I left. I went to her door the next day, I was twelve, I said the same thing I'd been saying for two weeks to myself, "my granny won't be here today she'll be dead" I told no one this premonition, I just held it inside.

My Mum opened the door and said your granny is dead. I started to weep, loudly, I loved her after all, I was the second last person to see her alive, she knew and I knew, she was leaving, the pocket money on the Thursday and the butter sandwich told it all.

As I matured, I became a single Mum I related to my granny over and over again. She was strong, but wobbly, like me, we both wondered "why me" on more than one occasion, but we both got busy with the business of carrying on, of being mighty, I look like her today. I try to do my granddaughter Jai's hair like granny used to do mine. We have the same battles. I just got luckier than her, I got a second love, a peaceful reprieve, a moment to rest. I hope my granny got that. I hope her children, her in laws and her grandchildren provided that for her.

She was my mighty granny - she did it all with her heart and soul.

GRAND CHILDREN

*B*eing a Nana is the best role in the entire world. I have relished in it, adored it, wallowed in it. I have found myself speechless with love, with joy, with the most intense emotions. I have felt tears run down my face of sheer joy at the miracle of each one of my grand children at birth.

I have four very precious grandchildren. Emily, Amy, Jai and Kieran. They each bring something different to the table, with their uniqueness and diversity.

Emily is confident. Willing to take risks, goes out of her comfort zone, tries new things. She is a beautiful painter, a trendy dresser, a lover of expensive perfume a loyal friend, a happy go lucky gem of a person.

Amy is quieter, she loves animals, will spend hours upon hours with her horses, her dog Trixie and cats Chole and Zoe. She thrives in structured routines, and predictable people. Amy is very good at photography, loves being on a farm and adored by both her parents. Amy is kind, thoughtful, honest, generous, considerate and talented.

Jai is much younger, she treasures her older cousins, her best friend Grace, playing games, pushing herself with all things athletic, she is honest and brave and very loving.

Kieran is my only grandson, he is busy, playful, curios, determined, funny. He loves his sister Jai, his parents and basketball. He loves making friends and he is cuddly and sweet. He has tons of energy, and has great self awareness for a six year old.

Some of my most heartfelt moments have been spent in their presence.

I cannot find the words to describe the depth of my love for them. When they walk through our front door they are met with the biggest smile and wide open arms. I cuddle them tightly with my hugs. Our house lights up when they're here, we get busy with going to the park or the mall depending on how old they are.

It is the most precious gift in life to have grandchildren. It's a pure honor to laugh with them and all their little antics. To watch them grow and enter different ages and stages of life, to see them achieve desired goals and to see them sit quietly contemplating their next move,

It's a glorious role it's bigger than my heart and my capacity of love, it's bigger than me, and my vocabulary, it's monumental, a treasure, a precious priceless gift to behold and I am eternally grateful for the privilege and the pleasure of being their Nana.

WE ARE THE LUCKY ONES

I was broken when I walked through the doors of AA. Inside I felt shattered, torn to pieces, terrified to drink, petrified not to. Minutes seemed like hours and hours seemed like days. The endless noise in my head wouldn't stop - the thoughts were overwhelming, disturbing. I bounced around the house like a junkie sitting standing laying down, up down all around. I'd try to watch something on tv but I couldn't concentrate Forget about reading I'd never get past the first few lines, nothing staying in the brain. It was baby steps. Get a sponsor, get to meetings, read the daily reflection, live a day at a time, pick up the 500 pound phone and call your sponsor. Little by little it began to sink in.

Once I worked the steps I started to become accountable, the days grew into weeks, the weeks turned into months, and the months into a year. With time came stability and the heartfelt attempt at making amends. I knew I had really hurt people when I drank. I lashed out at certain people with my high and mighty attitude.- hurting others with my quick attacks and flipping people off including my kids, sister in law, husband and friends. I needed to acknowledge those people with my sincere amends.

The rest was daily maintenance and reaching back to help the people coming in behind me. My emotional sobriety has been born in doing my work, healing my wounds, through my program and reaching out for therapy from outside agencies. I did some very heavy emotional therapy. EMDR which took me back to painful childhood experiences but healed and freed me to forgive, to nurture and love the little girl I was. I finally let her speak, scream, wail, convulse, hyperventilate, weep her pain out. She was finally heard, so she could finally heal.

By allowing all this to happen I became stronger emotionally more stable, More secure, more open, more honest, more real, more determined, more helpful, much much more willing.

Recovery is a process. It's a journey, it's a beautiful road with some twists and turns, some peaks and valleys, it's exciting and rewarding, it's daunting and confusing but it's worth every moment, every tiny feeble effort. The reward is becoming a mature parent, partner, friend, employee, sponsor, sponsee, Someone who can be forgiven today and has grace enough to forgive others.

This immense journey saves lives, saves relationships, saves jobs, saves families and saves friendships. We are the lucky ones, we found a program that has the tools to build lives from the ground up. We get second and third and fourth chances. We get to choose if we want this life and if we do then we pick up the tools and start working and chipping away at ourselves and one day we find we are participating in the world as functioning, emotional, wholesome, emotionally sober adults.

GUIDED BY GRACE

*T*his book has come from my heart onto these pages, it has been guided by grace, I have felt as though the words came through me, and linked together to make sentences, which built paragraphs, which resulted in stories of my life and my people, which will turn into a book.

It has been a life long dream to write a book. Until I sat down with the first couple of stories I didn't know it was going to be a memoir of short stories and poems. The writing was just unfolding at such a rapid pace through me, like it was all bursting to come out.

I attended a weekend workshop the weekend before I started writing. All the authors said to write every day and I have. Some days producing three stories a day. This process has been so freeing and rewarding. I have gained a beautiful friendship with my writing partner whom wishes to remain anonymous. My writing partners feedback has been invaluable, welcomed, desired, treasured, and appreciated. Merci my friend.

It is my greatest hope that my family and friends will buy this book, and that they will be lost in the writing, and renewed by the storytelling. There are some dark pieces in here, but isn't that what life is? Dark and light, ups and downs, painful and joyful. So I hope you find something in here that touches you deeply, that helps you relate, that invokes emotions and invites discussion.

The greatest compliments I have ever received regarding my writing, are these: Your writing is like a river it flows. My writing partner and You are a writer and a healer, also my writing partner. Can there ever be more "holy words" to the heart of a writer? I think not.

I have done the hard work of healing. This book would not be possible without the determination of working through the painful issues I lived through. It took courage, to go through the process of visiting these painful experiences again in therapy, but it's vital, so vital in the process of living a healthy life. I could not write these stories if I had not healed, if I had not done the heavy lifting of engaging the pain, and consoling it with compassion, love, warmth, and tenderness. Then and only then, could I write these stories without bitterness and resentment, without hatred and loathing. I wrote them with love, and I hope with understanding of the disease of alcoholism.

I have been guided by grace throughout my life, to live this life even the most challenging parts of it, and to now document it for you, my reader. Please enjoy this journey, laugh, cry, get angry, root for the characters, rejoice in the determination, and if you love it. Please pass it on through word of mouth or by buying one for a friend or relative.

HELP HOPE & HEALING

*I*n 2017 I found myself on my knees desperately seeking help. My husband Ian had just had a talk with me about my drinking and how concerned he was for me. He was so loving, caring, compassionate, initially my response was one of defensiveness, once I found out that the concern was coming from my son Josh my defensiveness quickly changed to shame, guilt and remorse. I made a decision to stay home from work, to go see my doctor.

It was early so I called in sick and went to lay down on my bed until the doctors office opened. I was laying in bed in a fetal position, weeping. I could not believe what I had put my family through. From my husband and kids, to my sister-in-law and her family. I was sick with guilt.

We managed to see the doctor that day. Ian stayed home with me, I told the doctor I thought I was an alcoholic, that I couldn't stop drinking, that I promised myself every morning I wouldn't drink again, but by three o'clock I was desperate for a drink. So the cycle would start all over again for another twenty four hours.

The doctor kept me off work and I went home to mope. I didn't know what to do. I reached out to a few friends, but I think they thought I was nuts, which I was. I paced around the house trying to function but failing.

Within the next week I found myself at the doors of AA I'd been guided there by a women from Women For Sobriety. That organization had folded in my community so she suggested s women's AA group along with attending an alcohol and drug treatment facility in our community the next day.

I went to the meeting and reached my hand out for help and suddenly all these women reached their hands back out to me. It was so touching, I felt safe, and suddenly I felt hope. One women took me out for coffee, bought me a big book, and told me to go to the same alcohol and drug treatment facility the next day, which I did.

The people at the facility were amazing. I saw a counselor and signed up for a day treatment program. I began to feel alive again. I was feeling so much hope that i was in the right places doing the right things.

The counseling revealed some chemical imbalances that I had been dealing with my whole life. These were ups and downs, my counselor was smart enough to recognize them and referred me to see the psychiatrist. I was placed on medication with one tweek and I have been so balanced since. I am so grateful for the opportunity to live a more stable existence.

Working the steps, restored me to sanity. Like step one admitting I was powerless over alcohol, acknowledging I was an alcoholic was easy and recognizing how unmanageable my life had become was glaringly obvious to me.

Step two Came to believe that a power greater than myself could restore me to sanity was simple. The group represented a power greater than me, until I could eventually believe in having a higher power.

Step three made a decision to turn my will and my life over to the care of God as i understood him. This was made much easier for me when it was explained that my will was my thoughts and my life is my actions. Doing big book studies along with my counseling provided me with healing. I am more whole today than I have ever been.

Step four taking a moral and fearless inventory, this step was easy in that I was very clear on my defects of character, I was selfish, envious, self centered, a gossiper, just to name a few.

Admitting them to someone else is step five so those and other defects were revealed.

Step six was becoming willing to have god remove these defects of character. I was very willing to have my defects removed to live a life without them.

Step seven Humbly asked him to remove these shortcomings. That's asking God to take them away Giving them over to God present challenges as I often take them back!

Step eight made a list of all people we had harmed. I harmed many, I could find some of them in step four.

Step nine Made amends to such people whenever possible except when to do so would injure them or others. Sometimes it's not wise to make an amends because it'll cause more harm than good. Sometimes i just can't because someone doesn't want to hear it. But the ones I can make amends to, provides so much healing, so much cleaning of my side of the street, so much relief, so much freedom. It's worth the hard work, the courage, the digging, the perseverance, the determination. It's so important to the healing of relationships, for seeing, owning, and acknowledging the damage I've done in the wreckage of my past. It's the least I can do to clean it up.

Step Ten is continued to take personal inventory and when we were wrong promptly admitted it. I try to practice this very promptly in my daily life.

Step Eleven sought through prayer and meditation to improve my conscious contact with God. By taking the "time to pray and meditate" I will gradually build a closer relationship with my Higher Power, which builds a much stronger spiritual connection for daily living

Step Twelve Having had a spiritual awakening as a result of these steps we carry this message to others and practice these principles in all our affairs. There is a spiritual awakening with working these steps, a realization of my love and a connection to something greater than myself. I carry the message when I welcome a newcomer, speak to a sponsee, or chair a meeting. I practice the principles by how I live my life, by being honest, open, sincere, generous, kind, open, caring, objective, real, sincere.

This program provided help, hope and healing, I did the work, the fellowship provided the support, love, guidance, caring and immense direction. My family stood by me every step of the way, providing unwavering love and support.

This is a solution to the problem of alcoholism I promise you. Do the work, dig deep, you'll have all the guidance, support, direction, love and inspiration you need. All you have to do is show up, and the rest will be revealed.

Lightning Source UK Ltd.
Milton Keynes UK
UKHW010811110123
415170UK00001B/86